W9-DAV-884

My Big Backyard

Lizards

Lola M. Schaefer

Heinemann Library
Chicago, Illinois

© 2004 Heinemann Library
a division of Reed Elsevier Inc.
Chicago, Illinois

Customer Service 888-454-2279
Visit our website at www.heinemannlibrary.com

Designed by Kim Kovalick, Heinemann Library; Page layout by Que-Net Media
Printed and bound in China by South China Printing Company Limited.
Photo research by Bill Broyles
Edited by Tameika Martin

08 07 06 05 04
10 9 8 7 6 5 4 3 2 1

Library of Congress Cataloging-in-Publication Data
Schaefer, Lola M., 1950-
    Lizards / Lola M. Schaefer.
        v. cm. – (My big backyard)
Includes bibliographical references (p.   ).
Contents: Are lizards in your backyard? – What are lizards? – What do lizards look like? – How big are lizards? – What do lizards feel like? – What do lizards eat? – What is something special about lizards? – How do lizards stay safe?
    ISBN 1-4034-5047-1 (hardcover) – ISBN 1-4034-5735-2 (pbk.)
    1. Lizards–Juvenile literature. [1. Lizards.] I. Title.
    QL666.L2S328 2004
    597.95–dc22

                                        2003021021

Acknowledgments
The author and publishers are grateful to the following for permission to reproduce copyright material:
p. 4 M. C. Chamberlain/DRK Photo; p. 5 Yva Momatiuk and John Eastcott/DRK Photo; p. 6 William Leonard/DRK Photo; pp. 7, 9, 13, 16, 18, 22, 24 John Sullivan/Ribbit Photography; p. 8 Jacques Denzer Parker/Index Stock Imagery; pp. 8, 21 Corbis; pp. 10, 11 Wayne Lynch/DRK Photo; p. 12 Stephen J. Krasemann/DRK Photo; p. 14 T. A. Wiewandt/DRK Photo; p. 15 John Cancalosi/DRK Photo; p. 17 Marty Cordano/DRK Photo; p. 19 Francois Gohier/Photo Researchers, Inc.; p. 20 McDonald Wildlife Photography/Animals Animals; p. 23 (t-b) Stephen J. Krasemann/DRK Photo, M. C. Chamberlain/DRK Photo, Corbis; back cover (l-r) Stephen J. Krasemann/DRK Photo, Corbis

Cover photograph by John Sullivan/Ribbit Photography

Every effort has been made to contact copyright holders of any material reproduced in this book. Any omissions will be rectified in subsequent printings if notice is given to the publisher.

Special thanks to our advisory panel for their help in the preparation of this book:

Eileen Day
Preschool Teacher
Chicago, IL

Kathleen Gilbert
Second Grade Teacher
Round Rock, TX

Sandra Gilbert
Library Media Specialist
Fiest Elementary School
Houston, TX

Jan Gobeille, Kindergarten Teacher
Garfield Elementary
Oakland, CA

Angela Leeper
Educational Consultant
Wake Forest, NC

Pam McDonald
Reading Teacher
Winter Springs, FL

Contents

Some words are shown in bold, **like this.**
You can find them in the picture glossary on page 23.

Are Lizards In Your Backyard?

You might see a lizard in your backyard.

It could be sitting on a rock.

Lizards live in warm places all over the world.

They live in trees, bushes, and rocks.

What Are Lizards?

scales

Lizards are **reptiles**.

Scales cover their bodies.

Lizards are cold-blooded.

Their body temperature is the same as the air around them.

What Do Lizards Look Like?

Lizards have long, thin bodies.

They have short legs.

Lizards can be many different colors.

Some colors are bright!

How Big Are Lizards?

Lizards can be many sizes.

Some are as small as your finger.

Some lizards are as long as a lunch table.

It can weigh as much as a person.

What Do Lizards Feel Like?

claws

Scales on lizard skin feel rough.

The **claws** on their feet feel sharp.

A lizard sitting in the sun would feel warm.

A lizard sitting in the shade would feel cool.

What Do Lizards Eat?

Some lizards eat plants.

They eat leaves, fruits, and flowers.

Some lizards eat bugs.

Large lizards can eat big animals.

What Is Something Special About Lizards?

Some lizards change color.

They can look like the plants around them.

If a lizard loses part of its tail, it will grow back.

How Do Lizards Stay Safe?

Most lizards stay safe by hiding.

Their enemies cannot see them.

Many lizards shed a part of
their tail.

Then, they run from their enemies.

Are Lizards Dangerous To You?

Most lizards are not dangerous to people.

They will always try to run away.

Some lizards can be dangerous.

They may bite people if they
are afraid.

Quiz

What are these lizard parts?

?

?   **?**

Picture Glossary

claw
page 12
a sharp nail on the finger or toe
of an animal

reptile
page 6
a cold-blooded animal like a turtle
or a snake

scales
pages 6, 12
the skin on an cold-blooded animal
like a snake

Note to Parents and Teachers

Reading for information is an important part of a child's literacy development. Learning begins with a question about something. Help children think of themselves as investigators and researchers by encouraging their questions about the world around them. Each chapter in this book begins with a question. Read the question together. Look at the pictures. Talk about what you think the answer might be. Then read the text to find out if your predictions were correct. Think of other questions you could ask about the topic, and discuss where you might find the answers. Assist children in using the picture glossary and the index to practice new vocabulary and research skills.

 CAUTION: Remind children that it is not a good idea to handle wild animals. Children should wash their hands with soap and water after they touch any animal.

Index

Answers to quiz on page 22

scales

claw   tail

DATE DUE

APR 1 2 2008	
AUG 0 5 2008	
OCT 0 8 2011	
MAR 0 7 2013	
MAY 2 8 2013	

BRODART, CO. Cat. No. 23-221-003